Honest Abe

Paintings by **Malcah Zeldis**

Words by **Edith Kunhardt**

This book is Donated to the
East Haddam Free Public Library by

**The
East Haddam
Community
Lions**

 Greenwillow Books

An Imprint of HarperCollinsPublishers

jjB4n

With thanks to Philip B. Kunhardt, Jr.,
for checking the manuscript for accuracy—E. K.

The full-color artwork was prepared with gouache paints on paper.
The text type is ITC Cheltenham Book.

Honest Abe
Illustrations copyright © 1993 by Malcah Zeldis
Text copyright © 1993 by Edith Kunhardt
All rights reserved. Printed in Singapore.
www.harperchildrens.com

Library of Congress Cataloging-in-Publication Data
Kunhardt, Edith.
    Honest Abe / by Edith Kunhardt; pictures by Malcah Zeldis.
        p.   cm.
    "Greenwillow Books."
    Summary: A simple biography of the president who led the United States through a bloody civil war.
    ISBN 0-688-15838-2 (pbk.)
    1. Lincoln, Abraham, 1809–1865—Juvenile literature. 2. Presidents—United States—Biography—Juvenile
literature. [1. Lincoln, Abraham, 1809–1865. 2. Presidents.]
I. Zeldis, Malcah, ill.   II. Title.
E457.905.K86   1993   91-47191
973.7'092—dc20   CIP
[B]   AC

To my grandson, James Redden McDonough,
and to the memory of my friend Robert Bishop
—M. Z.

This book is lovingly dedicated
to my grandfather Frederick Hill Meserve
and my mother, Dorothy Meserve Kunhardt
—E. K.

Abraham Lincoln was born in Kentucky, in a log cabin. His parents, Thomas and Nancy Lincoln, were poor. His father worked hard as a carpenter and farmer, and his mother helped him in the fields. Neither his mother nor father could read or write.

Abraham had an older sister named Sarah. When he was old
enough to go to school, he and Sarah walked two miles to the
one-room schoolhouse. Children from every grade sat in the
same room. All the schooling Abraham Lincoln ever had added
up to one year. But he was eager to learn, and he taught himself.

When Abraham was seven, the family moved one hundred miles away, to Indiana. They packed up everything they owned on two horses and traveled through the wilderness. There were wolves and bears in the woods they had to cross.

The first year they were in Indiana, Abraham helped his father build a cabin. It had one room and a dirt floor. When it was finished, Abraham slept up in the loft. His mattress was a pile of dry leaves.

Two years later Abraham's mother died. Abraham played with his cousin Dennis, who had come to live with them, but nothing was the same.

Another year went by, and Thomas Lincoln left Abraham and Sarah
and Dennis alone in the cabin and went back to Kentucky.

Weeks later he returned with a new wife. Her name was also Sarah, but
Thomas called her Sally. She brought with her her three children and
all her furniture from her old home.

Abraham loved Sally, and she loved him. She got Thomas to put a
wooden floor in the cabin and to fix the leaky roof. Now eight people
lived in one room.

Sally helped Abraham to study at night. He read by firelight. He borrowed books and newspapers. He read about George Washington. He read the Bible. He wrote poems. He taught himself.

Abraham was growing strong and tall. His father hired him out to other farmers for twenty-five cents a day. He chopped down trees for firewood and split logs to make rail fences. He was a very good worker. Sometimes he jumped up on a tree stump and told funny stories and jokes. People loved listening to him.

Abraham almost always had a book in his pocket or in his hand. He even carried a book with him when he plowed the field. He would read while his horse was resting at the end of a corn row.

When he was nineteen years old, Abraham was six feet four inches tall.
He weighed more than two hundred pounds and was a powerful
wrestler and a swift runner.

Abraham worked on a flatboat on the Mississippi River. Flatboats
carried hogs and corn to market.

The boat traveled down the river to New Orleans. There Abraham saw slaves. These black people did not get paid for the work they did. White people owned them and could sell them. Abraham thought this was wrong.

Soon after Abraham got back from New Orleans, Thomas Lincoln moved his family to Illinois. And soon after that Abraham left home. He moved to New Salem, a small town in Illinois, where he worked in a store. After a while people began to come to the store just to hear Abraham tell stories.

People called him Abe or Honest Abe. Once a woman paid him six and a quarter cents too much. He walked three miles to find her and pay her back.

Abe had many jobs in New Salem. He was postmaster, delivered mail, and surveyed land.

Abe liked visiting courthouses and hearing the lawyers' arguments.
Many people came to him for advice. He decided to become a lawyer
himself. He studied hard. He worked at night, and in three years he
became a lawyer.

Abe moved to Springfield, Illinois, where he met Mary Todd. Mary was twenty-one years old. Abe was thirty. Mary was popular. She liked dancing and spoke French. Abe and Mary were married.

Abe wore a tall silk hat in which he kept bills, notes, and legal papers.
Sometimes when he took off his hat the papers fell on the ground.
Abe's office was in Springfield. But he also rode to small towns far out
on the prairie to help decide legal cases. He made many friends. He
ran for Congress and was elected.

A few years later Abe decided to run for the United States Senate. He ran against Stephen A. Douglas. Douglas believed that slavery should continue. Lincoln believed that slavery should end. Lincoln and Douglas traveled all over Illinois, debating each other. When the people voted, Douglas won, but the debates made Lincoln famous.

Lincoln and Douglas ran against each other again two years later. This time the contest was for the Presidency of the United States, and Lincoln won. Abe, Mary, and their three sons moved into the White House in Washington, D.C.

The boys loved the old house. They played in the attic, rode their pony
on the lawn, chased their goats through the halls.

Two weeks after Abraham Lincoln became President, the Civil War started. It was a war between the people who lived in the northern states, most of whom believed slavery should end, and the people who lived in the southern states, most of whom believed slavery should continue.

Almost two years passed. Thousands of soldiers had been killed in the
war, and the South seemed to be winning. In addition Willie, the President's
twelve-year-old son, died. It was at this difficult time that Lincoln
wrote the Emancipation Proclamation. This was a milestone on the road
to the final end of slavery. Two years later the Thirteenth Amendment
to the Constitution outlawed slavery in the United States forever.

The war continued. A terrible battle took place at the little town of Gettysburg, Pennsylvania. Thousands of soldiers were killed there.

Five months later President Lincoln went to the battlefield to dedicate a cemetery to those who had died. The speech he made, known as the Gettysburg Address, lasted only about two minutes but remains one of the most famous speeches in American history. He said that no one would ever forget the brave men who had died there and that "government of the people, by the people, for the people, shall not perish from the earth."

The war ended after more than four years. "I've never been so happy in my life," the President said.

Five days later President and Mrs. Lincoln went to the theater. As they watched the play, a man who was furious at the President for freeing the slaves crept up behind him and shot him in the head. The bullet went into his brain.

President Lincoln remained unconscious through the night. In the morning he died.

His body lay in a coffin in the White House, and many people cried.

A train took President Lincoln's body on the long trip back to
Illinois. Thousands of people stood by the tracks to say good-bye.
He was given a funeral in ten different cities along the way.
Finally the train reached Springfield, where he was buried.
Honest Abe was home.

The Gettysburg Address

Fourscore and seven years ago our fathers brought forth on this continent a new nation, conceived in liberty, and dedicated to the proposition that all men are created equal.

Now we are engaged in a great civil war, testing whether that nation, or any nation so conceived and so dedicated, can long endure. We are met on a great battlefield of that war. We have come to dedicate a portion of that field as a final resting place for those who here gave their lives that that nation might live. It is altogether fitting and proper that we should do this.

But, in a larger sense, we cannot dedicate—we cannot consecrate—we cannot hallow—this ground. The brave men, living and dead, who struggled here, have consecrated it, far above our poor power to add or detract. The world will little note, nor long remember, what we say here, but it can never forget what they did here. It is for us the living, rather, to be dedicated here to the unfinished work which they who fought here have thus far so nobly advanced. It is rather for us to be here dedicated to the great task remaining before us—that from these honored dead we take increased devotion to that cause for which they gave the last full measure of devotion—that we here highly resolve that these dead shall not have died in vain—that this nation, under God, shall have a new birth of freedom—and that government of the people, by the people, for the people, shall not perish from the earth.

The Life of Abraham Lincoln

FEBRUARY 12, 1809	Born in Hardin County, Kentucky.
NOVEMBER 1816	Family moved from Kentucky to Indiana.
OCTOBER 5, 1818	Mother died in Spencer County, Indiana.
DECEMBER 2, 1819	Father married Sarah Johnston in Elizabethtown, Kentucky.
MARCH 1, 1830	Family started migration from Indiana to Illinois.
JULY 1831	Moved to New Salem, Illinois.
APRIL 21, 1832	Chosen as captain in Black Hawk War.
AUGUST 4, 1834	Elected to Illinois State Legislature.
APRIL 12, 1837	Started to practice law in Springfield, Illinois.
NOVEMBER 4, 1842	Married Mary Ann Todd.
AUGUST 1846	Elected to U.S. House of Representatives.
NOVEMBER 2, 1858	Lost Senate election to Stephen A. Douglas.
MAY 18, 1860	Nominated for Presidency by Republican Party.
NOVEMBER 6, 1860	Elected President of the United States.
APRIL 12, 1861	The Civil War (also called The War Between the States) began.
JANUARY 1, 1863	Signed the Emancipation Proclamation.
NOVEMBER 19, 1863	Delivered the Gettysburg Address.
NOVEMBER 8, 1864	Re-elected President.
APRIL 9, 1865	The Civil War ended.
APRIL 14, 1865	Shot by John Wilkes Booth at Ford's Theater, Washington, D.C.
APRIL 15, 1865	Died, age 56.
MAY 4, 1865	Buried in Springfield, Illinois.